THE VOICE OF THE HEART

Poems by

Sara Lee Langsam

AMERISSIS PRESS

Langsam, Sara Lee
Voice of the Heart / Sara Lee Langsam.
Amerissis Press, 2021
email: langsalight@gmail.com

Trade paperback: 978-0-578-91341-4
Also available in Kindle and Epub versions.

1. God. 2. Poetry 3. Spiritual Path 4. Religion & Spirituality 5. New Age
6. Enlightenment

cover photo by Igor Zubkov/iStock photo

* back cover quotation: Thomas Moore, "Believe Me, If All Those
Endearing Young Charms" in *Stevenson and Moore, A Selection of Irish
Melodies,* 1808

Printed in the United States of America

Dedication

This book of poems is dedicated to the Ancient of Days and the one hundred and forty-four thousand.

Acknowledgements

My deep gratitude goes to Mark L. Prophet and Elizabeth Clare Prophet for introducing me to the reality, beauty and glory of the Higher World and its hidden mirror image in our inner world. Without them this book would not have been written.

To my editor, Patricia Robertson, and my book designer, Lawrence Didona, I express my gratitude for their continued efforts on my behalf.

I am grateful to my father and mother who taught me by example to strive to do your best in every endeavor.

To all my friends from whom I received the love, wisdom and good will from their hearts, I welcome and am grateful for your encouragement and your rejoicing in my victories.

LISTEN TO YOUR HEART
A *Modern-Day Psalm*

Listen to your heart
You will not go astray.
Its voice so soft yet clear
Shows you the true way.

Listen to your heart
It speaks in still of night.
Its gentle wisdom pure
Will set your life aright.

Listen to your heart
And not the ways of men.
In love it reaches out
To strengthen you again.

TABLE OF CONTENTS

POEMS

(Continued on next page)

From the Heart

A heart that is increasingly replete with love, wisdom, faith and good will is necessary to navigate the rocky shoals of our everyday existence.

These poems are offered to help the reader access the depths and heights of our lives — the depths we must probe and transcend so that we can fully realize the reality, beauty and glory of the Higher World.

The Heart of Love

Love is an immovable force
A pulsating whirlwind of light
Drawing unto itself
All hatred
And in its fiery center
Consuming all unlike itself
Until love alone remains
A tribute to eternity
Dwelling in the here and now.

Patterns of Loveliness

Beauty is found in
Patterns of loveliness,
Drawing the soul onward,
Healing wounds,
Inspiring to grandeur.

Pressing onward
The soul reaches the summit
Of ultimate reality.

Mercy

Mercy is a drop of rain
Upon a parched flower,
A rainbow of promise
To a weary traveler,
Sunlight warming a shivering child,
A fragrant breeze in a meadow.

Mercy is found in the heart
Of one who takes the time
To listen to a tale of woe
And extends the hand of comfort
To ease the pain.

Destiny

The wind is a song
Singing the fiery destiny of man
In a starry universe.

A Goblet of Life

Life is sipped from a goblet
One drop at a time.
Its holy purpose
Draws us to a knowledge
Of our place in Infinity.

Broken Silence

Sometimes
We speak too soon.
And the sound
Shatters
The delicate web
Of golden thread
Woven in the stillness.

Accusation

We put a halo around the villain
And angrily accuse the victim
Who by speaking out
Upsets the neatly ordered blocks
Of our existence.

The Evil Ones

Who did such a terrible deed?
The evil ones.
Without the celestial spark of conscience
Within the breast,
Their black hole of nothingness
Belches clouds of smoke,
Leaving a trail
Of bloody degradation
In its wake.

The Noble Heart

Follow the path of the noble heart.
It counts not the cost
Of upholding
The eternal standard of integrity
In the face of transient ridicule
And temporary risk.

Those who mock the righteous ones
Are left in the shadow
Of their ignominy
And must sooner or later
Taste the ashes of their folly.

Crossroads

You have arrived at a crossroads.
A step to the right
Leads to Life's treasures.
The left ends in
Pitfalls and snares.
Having lost precious time
You must retrace your footsteps.

Collusion

"There is no evil," they say.
In their willful refusal
To see the enemy
They fuse with him
And in the last days
Are judged accordingly.

O Beloved Motherland America

America
Precious cradle of liberty,
Nurturing your sons and daughters
To be defenders of freedom
For an oppressed humanity.

Many unaware of
This noble destiny
Laugh and make merry.
They do not see the shadow
Waiting to pounce
On the sleeping babe.

The Keeper of the Flame

O noble soul
You have walked the earth
Throughout the ages
Leaving footprints
In the sands of time,
Keeping the flame
For child humanity.

The torch is passed to us
Who keep the flame
For our posterity.

Growing Up

The baby bird
Pushed out of the nest
Too soon
Falls to the ground.

Once grown
It flies away
Lest its wings be clipped.

Choices

A sense of beauty
Separates darkness from light
Paving the way
For a return to perfection.

Thoughts and feelings
Like flowers in a garden
Must be tended.

A weed like a dark thought
Must be uprooted
For the good plants to flourish.

Patterns of Perfection

Hold fast
To patterns of perfection
Until they are ingrained
In your soul
And bring forth
After their kind.

Masks and Deceits

We look to free ourselves
From our masks and deceits.
Freedom comes from
Knowing who we really are
And reaching for the star
Of our Divine Origin.

Homeward Bound

The soul
On its homeward journey
Must step upon
The sharp stones of previous experience.

Each drop of blood
Draws the soul
One step closer
To its ultimate destiny.

Free Will

The soul is given
The gift of free will
To maké right choices
For its victory.

Each choice
Leads to
Freedom or enslavement.

The soul
Tutored by the heart
Learns to thread
The needle of caution
As it makes its way
Among the rubble of allure
And false promises.

The Masters

Unseen
Their presence is felt
By many
Who long to be
A link in the chain
Of hierarchy.

The Brotherhood

Their love
Holds a suffering humanity
Tenderly
As they seek to help all
Reach a finer outpicturing
Of their inborn promise.

Teacher

With outstretched arms
You help us to cross
The bridge of enlightenment
Joining the past to the future.

Compromise

Peace at any price
Betrays the honor of a nation
And leads its people
Into enslavement.

The Jealous Ones

Having betrayed the divine spark
They seek to nip the flower
In its bud
Before it blooms.

The Aspiring One

Your meritorious service
Over many lifetimes
Makes you worthy
To be contacted
By the Brotherhood.

Afterword

"In all the moving forces of universal love beheld by man, there is a Spirit, a Master Presence, that colors all life with grandeur, with beauty, with logic, at once in time and infinity. We know and we have become one with that Spirit—which is God." *

---

* Mark L. Prophet, in *"The Soulless One: Cloning a Counterfeit Creation,"* 1965, p. 146

Biography

Sara Lee Langsam taught high school Spanish and English as a Second Language in high school and elementary school. Words have always fascinated her and the beauty and meaning of life that can be captured in poetry.

She has written three books of poetry: *Angels and Fairies and Bright Rainbows,* (original edition), *Angels and Fairies and Bright Rainbows* (expanded edition), and *The Voice of the Heart.* She also has published two children's books—*Francis Bacon: England's True Prince* and *Francis and Anthony: Inseparable Brothers.* Her most recent book, *The Homeward Path,* includes both poems and essays.

Sara Lee's poems, essays, and children's stories portray on a subtle level the ideas and concepts she has learned in her lifetime of studying the world's many spiritual and religious traditions. The knowledge of these traditions and their role in our everyday life has given the author the opportunity through her books to share with others these vital life-enhancing concepts.

Also by Sara Lee Langsam:
THE HOMEWARD PATH
ESSAYS & POETRY

Do you find yourself stepping back from the hectic fray of everyday life and wondering what it is all about? Sometimes we are so caught up with the tumult of the world that we tend to forget who we are and why we are here. In a quieter moment we may ask ourselves, "Is this all that life has to offer us? There must be something more." You are not alone.

Over the centuries many people from all walks of life have asked themselves similar questions. People like Origen of Alexandria, St. Francis of Assisi, and Khalil Gibran.

In this book, through her essays and poetry, Sara Lee Langsam shares her experience of approaching these deeply-felt questions. Herein is a yearning to probe the mysteries of life, the greatest of which lies within ourselves.

Life is a journey which ultimately leads us home. These essays and poems can be read and used as a meditation. Welcome to the homeward path.

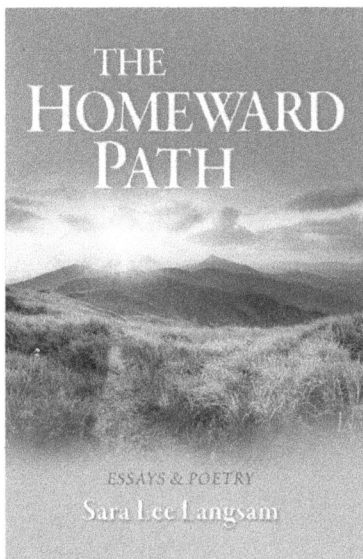

Available in paperback and Kindle formats
ISBN 978-0-578-85096-2
5.25 x 8 in./124 pages / $14